Assessing offenders' needs: assessment scales for the probation service

by

Rosamund Aubrey
Michael Hough

Criminal Policy Research Unit
South Bank University
London

A Research and Statistics Directorate Report

Home Office
Research and
Statistics
Directorate

London: Home Office

Home Office Research Studies

The Home Office Research Studies are reports on research undertaken by or on behalf of the Home Office. They cover the range of subjects for which the Home Secretary has responsibility. Titles in the series are listed at the back of this report (copies are available from the address on the back cover). Other publications produced by the Research and Statistics Directorate include Research Findings, the Research Bulletin, Statistical Bulletins and Statistical Papers.

The Research and Statistics Directorate

The Directorate consists of three Units which deal with research and statistics on Crime and Criminal Justice, Offenders and Corrections, Immigration and General Matters; the Programme Development Unit; the Economics Unit; and the Operational Research Unit.

 The Research and Statistics Directorate is an integral part of the Home Office, serving the Ministers and the department itself, its services, Parliament and the public through research, development and statistics. Information and knowledge from these sources informs policy development and the management of programmes; their dissemination improves wider public understanding of matters of Home Office concern.

First published 1997

Application for reproduction should be made to the Information and Publications Group, Room 1308, Home Office, Apollo House, 36 Wellesley Road, Croydon CR9 3RR.

©Crown copyright 1997 ISBN 1 85893 799 X
ISSN 0072 6435

Foreword

Scales for quantifying and recording offenders' problems and needs have been developed and used extensively by probation services in America and Canada over the last fifteen years. They are used to ensure that offenders are assessed effectively and consistently, and to measure how problems which are considered to be related to reoffending change during periods on supervision.

The project described here was commissioned to see whether simple and robust scales could be used in a British context, and whether probation officers found them useful and usable. It also looked at whether such scales could play a part in monitoring probation officers' performance.

The report concludes that such scales can be of considerable value in helping to structure assessment. It recommends the pay-offs will be greatest when the use of forms is properly integrated into the work process of probation officers. It suggests that the scope for using the scale as a performance indicator will be limited because of the gradual disclosure by some offenders of their offence-related problems.

These are key messages for probation services in England and Wales which are currently either buying-in North American assessment tools or developing their own scales locally.

CHRIS LEWIS
Head of Offenders and Corrections Unit
Research and Statistics Directorate

Acknowledgements

This research was commissioned by the Home Office Research and Statistics Directorate (RSD). We would like to thank several RSD members of staff – George Mair, Carol Hedderman, Julie Vennard and Chris May – for their help throughout the project. We are also grateful to John Kay (ACOP), Joe Kuipers (HM Inspectorate of Probation), Gay Leggett (NPRIE), Chris Hignett of the ILPS Research and Intelligence Unit and members of the Home Office Probation Unit for their guidance and support through the Steering Committee. Also to Ros Burnett of the Centre for Criminological Research, Oxford University, for advice in the early stages of the project.

The probation services which took part in the research were Middlesex, Inner London and Nottinghamshire and we would like to thank Graham Cross (Middlesex) and Brendan O'Keefe (ILPS) and their teams, David Webb (ILPS) and all the SPOs, POs and administrators in Nottinghamshire who were responsible for the organisation and completion of the needs assessment scales. Their feedback on the research was invaluable.

We are particularly indebted to various members of Nottinghamshire Probation Service: David Hancock (Chief Probation Officer) who committed his service to the research; John Kay (Assistant Chief Probation Officer) and Gill Francis (Research and Development Manager),who were unstinting in their support and advice even through the introduction of CRAMS. Administrators are the unsung heroes of research projects and Megan Dominy who undertook this task not only provided us with excellent support but was unfailingly helpful and cheerful in doing so.

ROSAMUND AUBREY
MICHAEL HOUGH

Contents

Summary

There is a steady accumulation of research about the factors associated with reconviction and about what forms of work with offenders on probation assist in reducing offending. There is thus a *prima facie* case for developing systems or structures which help to:

- improve and maintain the quality of assessment

- improve the consistency of assessment

- improve the allocation of resources

- document the needs of offenders under probation supervision

- assess the impact of supervision aimed at addressing offender needs.

This study has piloted three versions of a needs assessment scale for use by probation officers. The study has yielded findings both about the reception which such scales might receive amongst staff, and about the value of substantive results. The key points to emerge from the process of piloting the scales, and from feedback from probation officers about the scales, are:

- probation officers find no overwhelming difficulty in using needs assessment scales

- some find them useful as ways of structuring assessment

- many are less convinced about their potential for improving practice

- some found the classifications over-simplified

- there were some anxieties that scales might de-skill probation staff and erode their autonomy.

Some 1,500 forms were completed on almost 700 offenders at different stages in their supervision. Forms were completed more than once for almost 500 of the 700 offenders. Substantive findings about levels of need amongst this groups include:

- Problems with employment or finance were the most commonly identified problem in all three versions of the form.

- Problems associated with criminal friends and with intimate family relationships were commonly identified in all three versions.

- Problems with mental health, and with sexual, physical or racial abuse, were less often identified.

- Large minorities, or in one version, just over half, of offenders showed improvements in problems over time.

- Large minorities of offenders also showed no change.

- Large minorities of offenders showed apparent worsening of problems over time. This deterioration is best explained as an artifact of fuller disclosure over time, or as a product of variations in the definition of problems.

Policy implications

These findings have various implications for the development of needs assessment scales. They raise general issues about reconciling the demands for good-quality management information with the realities of professional practice, and more specific issues about the design of scales.

Implementing needs assessment scales

- Successful implementation of a national needs assessment scale will need carefully planned implementation, including an explanation of its purposes and advantages.

- The more that management information is produced as a by-product of everyday work processes, the more accurate and reliable it will be.

Designing needs assessment scales

- It is more realistic to conceptualise needs assessment scales in the probation setting as devices to structure assessment, rather than as diagnostic tools.

- There are strong arguments for using a simple binary classification system to measure need, in which officers have to decide if a need should be addressed in the course of supervision.

- Any national needs assessment scale should be compatible with local systems. This provides an added argument for a binary scoring system.

- Any assessment scale should avoid heavy selectivity in the items to be covered. Limiting a scale to a small number (3-6) of needs would skew practice towards addressing these needs.

- Whatever precise approach is taken to the assessment of need, it makes sense to ensure that this is properly integrated with assessing risk of reconviction.

- It is important to mount an empirical test of the proposition that risk of reconviction scales including needs variables are more precise than those which do not.

A "value-added" performance indicator

- There is an overwhelming case for collecting national information in a structured and consistent manner on the extent to which offenders' needs have been addressed.

- It may be possible to use such a scale to construct a performance indicator which sheds light on variations in performance across areas.

- However, problems associated with gradual disclosure of problems over time, as well as those associated with scale unreliability, will make it hard to interpret such a performance indicator.

- If such an indicator were used to distribute resources or rewards between probation areas or staff, manipulation of the scores would become rapidly institutionalised.

1 Introduction

This report presents the findings of a research project whose aim was to develop a needs assessment scale for the probation service. The requirement specified by the Home Office was to develop a simple and robust scale which would be of value both as an aid to professional practice in assessing offenders' needs, and as a source of management information. We were asked to pilot three scales of differing complexity, and in the light of results recommend how best to proceed. This introductory chapter describes the background to the project, and how we went about developing and piloting the three scales. Chapter 2 summarises the results of the pilot, and Chapter 3 offers our recommendations.

The requirement for a 'needs assessment scale'

Two central principles of probation practice are that offending is often rooted in the social and personal problems of offenders, and that addressing these problems can effectively reduce offending. People without jobs may have too much time on their hands and too little money, for example – an obvious precondition for some types of crime. Problems of drug dependency can often be implicated in property crime. Again, poor social skills and low levels of emotional control can often lock people into forms of violent crime. Identifying the nature of offenders' problems or needs and assessing whether these are related to the offending are pivotal tasks in probation supervision. The Home Office (1995) National Standards recognises this, in requiring proper needs assessment both when preparing Pre-Sentence Reports (PSRs), and when devising supervision plans for probationers.

Some probation areas have made better progress than others in formalising the process of assessing offender needs; few have got to grips with measuring the success of supervision in addressing these needs. Judging what it is that underlies someone's offending is certainly a highly complex process, and there is inevitably a large element of subjectivity and intuition to it. The process can be helped or hindered by diagnostic tools.

It is an open question how good the probation service currently is at assessing offender need. The work of HM Inspectorate of Probation shows that performance varies widely between officers and between services; and the Inspectorate has made frequent criticisms of the quality of supervision plans. Several researchers have reached similar conclusions. Burnett (1996) found that some areas had developed good assessment systems whilst others were much more 'hit or miss'. Some of the senior probation officers she interviewed were explicit both about the crudeness of the process and about differences between officers in consistency and style. Wilkinson et al. (1995) questioned whether the needs of women on probation are properly assessed. Roberts (1995) identified a clear need for the use of more rigorous and systematic forms of assessment to contain the individual idiosyncrasies of practitioners to a minimum. Similar conclusions were reached by Burnett:

> *A more systematic assessment of offending-related needs will enhance the accuracy and status of probation assessments, will foster optimum use of in-house and partnership specialists, and would facilitate integrated evaluation of the effectiveness of community supervision. (1996, p. 69)*

This body of work has prompted renewed interest within the probation service about allocation and assessment processes, and about the use of scales and scoring systems to assist these processes. In the light of Burnett's findings, the Home Office ran a series of regional seminars to enable senior probation managers to examine ways of improving procedures for assessing offenders and allocating them to officers.

How successful probation supervision is in addressing offenders' needs is an even greater unknown. Whilst there is a steady accumulation of research about the service's ability to reduce reoffending or reconviction (see McGuire, 1995, for various reviews), there is an almost total absence of information about the mechanisms by which these reductions are achieved. There is thus a *prima facie* case for developing systems or structures which help to:

● improve and maintain the quality of assessment

● improve the consistency of assessment

● improve the allocation of resources

● document the needs of offenders under probation supervision

● assess the impact of supervision aimed at addressing offender needs.

The reasons for doing so are partly to improve the quality of practice and partly to ensure accountability to probation management, paymasters and tax-payers. Any public service is required not only to perform effectively but also to demonstrate that it is earning its keep. In doing the latter, it has to be able to demonstrate both the *nature* of the job it is tackling and its *success* in doing so.

The service's performance in addressing need is of particular interest to the Home Office, as provider of 80 per cent of probation funds. In supporting this study, the Probation Unit wanted to know how feasible it would be to develop a measure of the 'value added' by probation supervision, which would allow the development of more focused performance indicators. In an ideal world, the measure would summarise average levels of need amongst offenders in a probation area at the start of supervision and on completion. A comparison of the 'before and after' figures would offer a pointer to what the service was achieving with its caseload.

A final but fundamental dimension in developing systems for assessing needs relates to the obligations and responsibilities which the service has towards the offenders it supervises. As a probation officer told Burnett (1996), 'Probation officers do exercise an awful lot of power in choosing what to offer.' An agency whose job is to offer help under conditions of coercion has some obligations to those whom it aims to help – not least to ensure that it is operating with equity.

Needs, problems and risk of reoffending

'Needs' and 'problems' are different sides of the same coin.[1] If an offender's unemployment is contributing to offending, then employment is a *need* and the unemployment is a *problem*. Needs – as distinct from wishes, entitlements or rights – are defined, often only implicitly, by reference to function. Basic needs, for example, are those which have to be met *to stay alive*. Emotional needs are (arguably) those which have to be met *to retain psychological equilibrium*. In the case of probation work as currently organised, offenders' problems reflect needs only if their resolution *reduces the risk of reoffending*, or brings some related advantages to the community. Some of the tensions in probation work stem directly from the application of this narrow criterion. Should a probation officer try to address an offender's poverty, for example, or poor housing, if these are unrelated to the probationer's offending or other anti-social behaviour?[2]

---

1   Whether either term is especially helpful in the process of empowering offenders is a question which concerned the project steering group. The term 'predicament' is arguably less perjorative and pathologising - but not a realistic alternative.
2   It is beyond our scope to debate this, though the answer implicit in, e.g., the 1995 National Standards is that such offenders should have no more or less access to the relevant services than non-offenders facing similar economic or housing problems.

Needs also have to be defined by reference to the resources available to resolve them. As folk-wisdom puts it, "If there's no solution, there's no problem". This implies, for example, that in areas where unemployment is endemic, the payoff in identifying employment training amongst an offender's needs may be smaller than in an area with extensive employment opportunities; and where psychiatric services diagnose an offender as having an untreatable personality disorder, the scope for probation intervention may also be limited. (In saying this, we would not want to belittle the frustrations of working with offenders with problems which can be identified but not addressed.)

Needs assessment scales and professional judgement

Needs assessment scales vary in complexity and in their relationship to professional judgement. They can serve three distinct functions. They can:

- *structure* professional judgement in assessing need

- supplement professional judgement in *diagnosing* need

- supplement professional judgement in *diagnosing risk of reoffending*.

Most needs assessment scales used in this country serve only the first function, of structuring judgement. Checklists focus officers' judgement on particular dimensions of need; for each dimension, they require a judgement to be made about the presence – or sometimes intensity – of need. Beyond this, however, they add nothing to the diagnostic process.

Some scales go further than this, supplementing the diagnostic process. Assessing offence-related needs and assessing risks of reoffending are inter-related but discernibly separate processes. Scales can help in both processes. There are innumerable scales devised by clinical psychologists, for example, for diagnosing psychiatric or social problems. And the probation service has extensive experience of predictive scales identifying risks of custody (in the 1980s) and risks of reconviction (in the 1990s). At the time of writing, the Home Office's Offender Group Reconviction Scale (OGRS) was being finalised.

These scales are usually actuarial devices enabling classification of a person on the basis of a small number of known (or easily ascertainable) characteristics. They are derived from statistical analysis of (usually large) samples of people, to identify what characteristics differentiate between those with the target attribute, and those without it.

The best examples of statistically derived diagnostic scales within probation are concerned with predicting reconviction rates (see Kemshall, 1996 for a review). These combine information about the offender's crime, criminal history, age, sex and (sometimes) 'social' variables such as employment, housing and substance misuse, to yield a probability of the offender getting further convictions. Whether such predictive scales can outperform professional judgement is an empirical question. There is some evidence that they can (see Kemshall, 1996). A more relevant test is whether people make more accurate judgements with the help of a statistical predictor than without. Typically, a reconviction scale tells an officer that the offender belongs to a sub-group of whom x per cent are reconvicted. The officer has to judge whether the offender is one of the x per cent who will be reconvicted, or the 100 - x per cent who will not. For example, a scale may place a young car thief with five previous convictions in a high-risk category, with a 75 per cent probability of reconviction in two years: it is then a matter of professional judgement to assess whether or not the offender will turn out to be amongst the 25 per cent who will not be reconvicted. By contrast, an adult sex offender with no previous convictions will probably emerge with a low risk of reconviction – perhaps in the region of 20-30 per cent – but it will still be of critical importance for the supervising probation officer to assess accurately whether the offender is one of the minority who will reoffend and be reconvicted.[3] As Copas said about using the Home Office's Offender Group Reconviction Scale when writing PSRs:

> the scale can .... be no more than an aid to the judgement of probation officers .... it cannot be a substitute for that judgement. A PSR may properly reflect a different assessment of risk from that to which the scale alone might point, as a result of the report writer's assessment of relevant information about the offender's circumstances or background. (Copas, 1994).

Statistically-based needs scales have been less thoroughly developed than reconviction scales within probation. There is, of course, a great diversity of scales developed by clinical psychologists to measure problems, but many of these are not particularly appropriate to the probation setting. The context in which assessments are made sometimes makes it impossible to deploy complicated 'pencil-and-paper' tests. Especially when preparing PSRs, there is limited time and often limited commitment on the part of the offender, whose ability to complete scales may also be limited. These considerations are less applicable when a supervision plan is being drawn up at the start of an order, and even less applicable in those areas which have set up specialist assessment units to do this work.

Work on needs assessment has been done mainly in North America, where

---

3   The value of actuarial scales which rely on *reconviction data is limited, of course, where there is a large gap between reoffending rates and reconviction rates. Sex offences provide a good example.*

scales have been used in conjunction with the assessment of risk for almost 20 years. The needs scales typically comprise lists of the main problems experienced by offenders such as unemployment, drug and alcohol misuse, mental health and personal relationships. Officers score each need in some scales simply as present or absent; in others they score for the intensity of need. And the most complex also attach differing weights to different types of problem – unemployment, for example, might score higher than homelessness.

The Wisconsin Correctional Services developed its risk/need classification system in 1979. The system listed 11 risk items and 12 needs. Each item was assigned a weighted score. The two sets of scores were totalled to identify low, medium or high in terms of risk and need. The higher score of the two determined the level of supervision for an offender. Needs and risk factors were identified from a small sample of 250 probation and parole cases. The risk scale was later evaluated for its validity in predicting risk of recidivism, though the needs were not. The use of Wisconsin-type risk/needs scales spread rapidly; by 1981 over 50 correctional services in the US and Canada were using them.

One Canadian scale which has attracted attention in this country is the LSI-R (Level of Service Inventory – Revised). This was originally developed by the Ontario Ministry of Correctional Services in the early 1980s, but has been subject to recent revision (Andrew and Bonta, 1995). This combines risk and needs factors together, to yield a single score indicating both risk of reconviction and the level of supervision required.[4] Sub-components of the scale can be separated out – sometimes confusingly referred to as 'risk' and 'need' elements. Completion of the scale takes around 45 minutes; a structured interview is carried out, and the answers to 54 questions are transferred onto a form from which scores can readily be calculated. Scoring is very simple: each positive answer scores one, and all positive scores are then summed. The scale attaches different weights to each dimension of need, by the simple procedure of asking more questions about needs which are heavily related to risk of reoffending. The weighting system has been devised not by actuarial analysis, but by meta-analysis, extrapolating from a large number of research studies which examine predictors of criminal behaviour (Sutton and Davies, 1996).

Needs assessment scales are now quite widely used in this country. Most probation services use a checklist of needs when preparing pre sentence reports (PSRs) and around half monitor social circumstances at the start and end of supervision. For example, ILPS uses a simple tick-box system for PSR preparation. Essex Probation Service has a more elaborate system in which needs are scored on a five-point scale at different points in the supervision

---

4   In keeping with the 'risk' and 'need' principles – cf Andrews et al., (1990) – which constitute the probation equivalent to the emergency medical assessment process of *triage*.

process. Hereford & Worcester has retained the tick-box system, but includes columns for planned intervention and reassessment; and the form is underpinned by guidance in the form of an Assessment Framework document. Those areas which have adopted the Northumbria computerised case management system have the facility to record at least 16 different types of need at three points in the supervision process; the scoring is currently binary.

Dimensions of need

There is clear evidence (e.g. Gendreau et al., 1995; Farrington, 1994) that persistent offending[5] is commonly associated with many factors, some of the main ones being:

- low family income

- poor housing

- an unstable job record

- poor educational attainment

- delinquent family or friends

- misuse of drugs and alcohol

- mental disturbance

- previous experience of violence or abuse

- a remote father (not necessarily an absent father)

- harsh and erratic discipline (at home or at school).

Evidence is more scarce that these associations are causal, but in our view, this is more a reflection of the difficulties of establishing causal links than of the impossibility of constructive work with offenders. Research on these factors is beginning to establish what sort of supervision programmes have the best chance of success (cf Lipsey, 1991, Losel, 1995). One can envisage the possibility of a totally 'research-driven' list of needs, all of which would be demonstrably related to offending and demonstrably amenable to probation intervention. For the time being, however, this is clearly more an aspiration than a reality. Deciding the range of salient needs on which probation work should focus remains a matter for professional judgement and theory.

---

5   There are, of course, some forms of crime whose offenders typically bear no resemblance to this profile - most obviously white collar crime.

The present study

The study's brief was to pilot needs assessment scales of differing complexity, and to make recommendations about the best balance to strike between complexity and usability. The work was set in the Nottinghamshire, Middlesex and Inner London Probation Services (ILPS). Our work was guided by a steering group drawn from the Home Office Probation Unit, the Research and Statistics Directorate, HM Inspectorate of Probation, Association of Chief Officers of Probation (ACOP), National Probation Research and Information Exchange (NPRIE) and participating services. We took as our starting point the revised Manitoba scale, as being one which had been exposed to at least a degree of validation, whilst remaining a simple instrument (Bonta et al., 1994). We modified this by varying the number of needs dimensions and varying the complexity of the scoring system.

We also made appropriate adjustments to the language used, anglicising and simplifying where possible. These three models were then pre-piloted with senior and main grade probation staff in two services and the research manager in one of the services which had agreed to take part in the full scale pilot. Substantial modifications were made with some needs being redefined, others added and the descriptions of needs further reworded. The resultant three models are at Appendix A.

It had originally been envisaged that the simplest of the three scales should concentrate only on three categories of need, felt to be the most salient in probation work. (Problems associated with employment, accommodation and substance misuse were canvassed as possibilities.) However, it rapidly became clear that such a reductionist scale had little chance of being piloted, let alone used in earnest. We thus ended up with three models focusing on the following needs:

- academic/vocational skills

- employment

- accommodation

- financial management

- social skills

- mental health

- friends/associates

- partner/family relationships

- racial/sexual/physical abuse

- drug misuse

- alcohol misuse

- physical health.

The Simple Version comprised the full list of 12 needs, requiring officers to score each need as 0 or 1. The Intermediate Version required officers to score each need as 0, 1 or 2; it combined drugs and alcohol as 'substance misuse', and dropped physical health. The Complex Version worked with the full list of 12 needs, and again required needs to be assessed on a three-point scale. However, it attached varying weights to different needs. For example, high levels of drug misuse scored six, whilst high physical illness scored only two. All models had a space for probation officers' comments.

Following a decision by senior management, all probation teams in Nottinghamshire took part in the project. In Middlesex and ILPS participating teams were identified by a process of calling for volunteers. One team put itself forward in Middlesex and two in ILPS – though one of these subsequently dropped out. In Nottinghamshire each of the three versions was used by city, urban and rural teams – to ensure that all three versions were piloted under varying conditions. The Intermediate Version was piloted in the teams in Middlesex and ILPS.[6]

All participating officers were asked to complete scales for all offenders on their caseload. Offenders with combination orders as well as probation orders were included in the research.[7] In Middlesex, officers completed forms three times: first, on a pre-pilot version, then in January 1996 and in mid-1996. In ILPS, forms were completed in early 1996 and again in mid-1996. In Nottingham, officers completed their first set of forms in early 1996; second and third sets were completed after three and six months. (It took longer than anticipated to set up the research and consequently there were variations in when the first assessments were completed.) The Middlesex and ILPS teams and the majority of Nottinghamshire teams supervise on a one to one basis, but other teams in Nottinghamshire work in a 'shared' system and in these cases the assessment was usually completed by the duty officer.

---

6   The Intermediate Version as piloted in Middlesex and ILPS had an additional category separated from the main list of needs which asked probation officers to judge an offender's motivation not to re-offend.

7   CSOs were not covered, as addressing offender needs is rarely a central part of CSO work.

In ILPS and Middlesex, the researchers explained the rationale of the project, and explained to officers how the exercise was to be conducted. A more formal process was followed in Nottinghamshire. Before piloting, there was a series of briefing meetings for SPOs and probation officers where the ACPO responsible for research and the Research and Development Manager explained the Service's commitment to the research, how it fitted in the national and local perspective and how it would be managed. Officers had brought case files with them and were able to complete first assessments so any teething problems were dealt with immediately.

Feedback from Nottinghamshire officers was collected both by means of a structured questionnaire and using group discussions - one for each version. A more informal process was followed in the other two sites. In assessing the scales, we used the following criteria:

- ease of use

- usefulness as a diagnostic tool for probation officers

- how they could be integrated into probation officers' work

- how they could be integrated into a computerised case management system

- usefulness to probation service management.

2 Results

This chapter presents the results of the pilot project. It comprises three types of finding:

● what we have learnt from the process of piloting the scale

● feedback from main-grade and senior probation officers

● analysis of the content of the forms themselves.

Lessons learned from the process of piloting

Piloting scales as a research exercise is clearly different from implementing them 'for real', but some lessons can be learnt from the process of mounting the study – even if the information comes from a somewhat oblique angle.

The relationship between management information and professional practice

We encountered various problems in administering the pilot. Some teams which originally agreed to take part found that they were unable to keep to the timescales required by the research, and had to drop out. For those who did take part, completing the forms was often an unwelcome chore, which was done mainly because SPOs or senior managers were backing the study. Some officers needed prompting to provide their returns. Although the level and quality of returns was eventually high, this was achieved by calling on the goodwill of probation officers and the support of SPOs and senior managers.

In part, our problems arose because the study was launched at an inauspicious time. We were asking for cooperation at a time when budget reductions and policy changes conspired to create a climate of uncertainty and anxiety. We would not want to labour the point. Plenty of officers reacted positively both to the concept of a needs assessment scale, and to its practical value (for example, when interviewing offenders). But our judgement is that if a needs assessment scale were introduced *first and foremost* as a means of collecting management information, the quality of the resultant information would be low unless it was accompanied by elaborate - and costly - quality control systems.[1]

The quality of management information can be maintained in the long term in two ways. One can either set up systems of *quality control* - as had to be done for our study - to ensure that people comply with the processes for creating the information; or else one can design processes in line with *quality assurance* principles which are likely to yield accurate information in the first place. The latter approach is more likely to yield consistently accurate information, at a lower cost.

In practice one of the surest ways to create processes for collecting accurate management information is to ensure that it is created as a by-product of core operations. In relation to needs assessment scales, this implies that the processes of assessing probationers, negotiating a supervision programme with them and recording these processes should be properly integrated and interwoven. For example, it might be realistic to think in terms of a scale or checklist which:

● helped officers structure assessment

● provided a tool for negotiating supervision programmes

● provided an easy means of recording the outcome

● and yielded useful management information as a by-product.

Such an integrated system stands a chance of yielding reliable management information without the need for persistent chasing by supervisors. We shall return to the issue of securing user support when we consider the feedback from individual officers later in this chapter.

Workload pressures

Some of the problems we encountered in getting teams to take part in the project seemed to arise because of increased workload pressures. An extra form to complete was one form too many. Even though caseloads have actually fallen over the last few years, we picked up a clear sense that officers felt under greater pressure than ever. Though we have no evidence, we believe that more work is probably been done with fewer, but more demanding offenders. Certainly the proportion of high-risk offenders under

---

1 One of the areas actually used a checklist which according to their R & I department failed to produce accurate or reliable information precisely for lack of such control systems.

probation supervision has been growing since the late 1980s. And new working practices, as set out in the National Standards in particular, require offenders to attend 12 appointments with their probation officer within the first three months of their order and six in the following three months. If workload pressures have increased, overlaying this trend has been the introduction of systems to ensure greater accountability to local managers. Not surprisingly, therefore, we encountered a poor climate in which to introduce a new form of monitoring.

Needs assessment scales and the development of IT

It became obvious to us in the process of mounting the pilot that information technology was rapidly changing working practices within the service. The movement away from paper filing systems is well under way. In Nottinghamshire, a version of the Northumbria case management system was being implemented by the time our fieldwork was ending. Any needs assessment scale either has to be readily incorporatable into a computerised case management system, or else it must be readily reducible into a form which can be so included. Our recommendations have been shaped in part by the probability that needs assessment scales are likely to be completed in a paper-free environment within a few years – regardless of whether they form part of a national case recording and management system (CRAMS).

Feedback from probation officers

We collected feedback from main-grade and senior probation officers in three ways: informally; in formal group discussions; and – in Nottinghamshire – via a short questionnaire which was completed by 29 officers.

The pros and cons of using needs assessment scales

There were mixed feelings among officers as to whether needs assessment scales were 'a good thing'. On the positive side, some officers:

- argued the case for a more systematic and consistent approach to assessment

- thought this would yield dividends in terms of consistency and equity

- found the scale useful as a practical aid

- were positive about using assessment scales with their clients

- said forms could legitimise the inevitably awkward questions which often have to be raised with offenders during interviews.

Others were less convinced, and the reasons are worth exploring in some detail. Various reasons were given for not needing or wanting the scales. Some probation officers saw assessment scales as a tool which might de-skill them, substituting a crude diagnostic tool for their professional judgement. They saw the development of the scales as part of a process of change – emanating largely from the Home Office – which had the effect of eroding their autonomy and professionalism.

Linked to this was a sense that scales would be redundant, because assessments were already being carried out in a professional manner; and some expressed disquiet at the implication that they were not already assessing needs competently or consistently. Many argued persuasively that assessment was a complex skill – or even art – which stood to gain little from such a crude and simple device. However, SPOs and senior managers tended to argue that there was obvious inconsistency in assessing and monitoring and that this raised issues of both equity and effectiveness.

Several officers objected to the reductionism involved in forcing people into categories. The scales attempted to illustrate the different levels of need by including descriptors in each box (e.g., for the dimension of financial management, the highest level of need carried the descriptor 'severe difficulties, debts, County Court judgements etc'). Officers complained that categories often failed to fit the client, and that the scale could not begin to capture the complexity of the situation.

There are two other factors which may underlie anxieties about needs assessment scales – though unsurprisingly, nobody articulated these. On the one hand there may be some resistance to any initiative which renders officers' effectiveness more transparent and assessable. And on the other, systems which identify discrete needs may be regarded as hastening the transformation of the probation role from generic case worker to case manager.

There were few obvious characteristics distinguishing sceptics from supporters. Some of those who valued the scale were recent staff. We cannot say whether inexperience or other factors underlay this, though others with 15 or 20 years' service also expressed enthusiasm for the scales. Generally, however, long-serving main-grade officers were more negative both about using the scale and about its potential usefulness than either less experienced officers or SPOs.

Check list or diagnostic tool?

As discussed in Chapter 1, needs assessment scales can vary in complexity from a simple checklist to a statistically validated diagnostic tool. The former can help structure assessment, but beyond this does little to help officers judge where offenders lie on any given dimension of need. The latter can supplement professional judgement. One implication of feedback from officers is that the very simplicity of a checklist stands in its favour, as no-one could construe it as a substitute for their professional judgement. This is not to suggest that opposition to more sophisticated diagnostic systems would be implacable. But it is clear that any service proposing to implement such a system will have to convince staff that it is intended as an adjunct to professional judgement, and not a substitute for it.

The value of management information

Most probation officers could see the potential for management information which could document the extent of need within their caseload, and point to probation achievement in addressing offenders' needs. (They were sceptical that this would result in more resources however.) Not surprisingly, SPOs were more attuned to the potential value of management information generated by a needs assessment scale – particularly when they saw the profile of needs of offenders on their team's caseloads. (It is of relevance here that HM Inspectorate of Probation's reports have commented on the under-use by senior probation officers of aggregate data to assess their teams work.)

The right dimensions of need?

Overall, officers seemed to think that we had settled on an adequately comprehensive list of needs. Some modifications were suggested:

- employment should be described as employability. This would bring in consideration of whether an offender needed vocational education/training or re-training or whether literacy and numeracy were a barrier to gaining employment. It could be a way of countering scepticism about scope for finding jobs for offenders in areas were unemployment is endemic

- racial, sexual and physical abuse should be separated into two categories; racial abuse and sexual and physical abuse. They are qualitatively different and require different interventions.[2]

---

2   We envisage that a positive score on physical or sexual abuse would imply that this was a problem which *currently* needed addressing, even if the abuse had occurred in the distant past.

- life skills: social skills were included in all three models, but probation officers asked *how do you tell someone they have got poor social skills?* It may be more appropriate to include as a need life skills which could encompass anger management, parenting, assertiveness, social skills etc.

- substance misuse (as in the Intermediate Version) was less preferable than disaggregated problems of drug and alcohol misuse (as in the other versions). The differences in legal status of alcohol misuse and most drug misuse, and the often divergent treatment responses made it unhelpful to conflate the two problems

- mental health would be more appropriately described as mental disturbance, in line with the NACRO Advisory Committee's broad definition (NACRO, 1993). This would encompass serious mental health problems covered by the Mental Health Act 1983 and minor disturbances such as bereavement exacerbated by stress

- a blank box should be included for probation officers to describe the needs of a particular offender – e.g. bereavement/loss; special educational needs or stress (which probation officers and offenders may not wish to categorise as a mental health problem)

- consideration should be given to including care responsibilities either for children, relations or non-relatives.

Some officers suggested that the scales were not especially consistent with the focus on offending behaviour which current practice was increasingly favouring. Most obviously, none of our categories of need related to those cognitive difficulties which are often addressed in cognitive-behavioural programmes.

Scoring the seriousness of needs

Most officers reported that it was often difficult to fit clients into specific categories of need. Often offenders fell between levels of need as indicated by our descriptors – and sometimes the descriptors failed completely to capture the essence of the offender's problem. The problems were more marked when officers had to choose between three levels of need (as in the Intermediate and Complex Versions) than for the Simple Version, where they had to make a yes/no decision. Some thought that assigning offenders to one of three levels of need was an exercise in spurious precision. In discussion, most favoured a binary model.

Another form of difficulty emerged in assessing inter-related needs. Officers offered examples of substance misuse causing employment problems and financial difficulties, for example. It was unclear how offenders should be scored on interlinked needs, and guidance would clearly be needed on this as part of implementation. Some officers favoured a field on the form for noting the presence of 'nested needs'.

It will be remembered that the Complex Version included a system of weighted scores – reflecting judgements on the perceived degree of risk associated with each need.[3] The reason for including this was to assess whether this caused practical difficulties or was in any way distracting. No-one reported any related problems, and only a very small proportion of forms had 'illegal' scores entered on them. Not surprisingly, no-one found the weighted scoring system as useful or relevant, as they were not asked to make any decisions based on offenders' total needs score.

Officers also raised problems about unmeetable need. Some needs cannot be addressed either because of variation in local provision or because of the nature of the need. For example, personality disorder is not considered treatable; some disabilities may be chronic and nothing more can be done to address the specific problem. (Whether nothing really can be done depends, of course, on the range of resources to which the service has access – which can be extended by effective inter-agency partnerships.)

Assessing improvement

Our starting point in designing the forms was that a scale with three (or more) levels of need would be more sensitive to changes in offenders' circumstances than a binary system. Probation officers commented that progress was often slow and the crudity of both a two- and a three-point scale did not allow for gradual progression. As one officer said, "Our clients don't go from A to Z, but to some point in between." In other words, progress might often be made in tackling a serious problem, without it being reduced to a minor or insignificant problem.

A more serious drawback to the measurement of improvement is that offenders do not disclose all their needs at PSR stage, or even at the start of an order. The real level of need sometimes emerges only after the first few weeks - or even months - of supervision. By then, officer and offender may have established a degree of trust; equally, the officer may be in a much better position to corroborate (or question) the offender's claims, and to challenge statements and attitudes. This deferred disclosure creates problems of practice, on the one hand, about how to meet offenders' needs

---

3   Our scoring system was partly informed by Canadian research and partly by 'commonsense'.

when they have already received their share of probation attention. On the other hand, it also creates problems about assessing progress. Simply comparing their scores on a needs assessment scale at the start and mid-point of supervision will often reveal an apparent deterioration. Empirical evidence on this is presented in the final section of this chapter.

Terminology

Officers were often critical about the terminology used to describe needs. The language was criticised at various points for being stigmatising, patronising, blaming or pathologising. The criticisms were made partly with practicalities in mind - that offenders would often see the form as it was being completed. Clearly it is important that any such scale should not cut across any supervision strategies aimed at empowering clients or building their self-esteem.[4]

Ease of use and accuracy

It was obvious from comments by officers on the needs assessment forms that not all the needs listed were fully assessed. Academic qualifications were most often not known, but officers also commented that other needs were unknown. There was sometimes insufficient information on which to base a judgement, either because this information had not been collected, or because of doubts over its reliability.[5] Some officers took a more tightly instrumental view than others of whether a problem was an offence-related need. For example, some noted that literacy was not an issue because the offender either had no problem finding work or was not looking for work, because of child care responsibilities.

The other major criticism was that the needs assessment forms did not have an action column for officers to record how the identified need was to be addressed. Including space for this on the form might well make it a more useful and usable document.

Despite all the criticisms mentioned above, the majority of probation officers found all three models easy to use. There were various criticisms about design and layout, but overall the format and concept were regarded as unproblematic.

Summary of officers' preferences

Taking into account all feedback from main-grade and senior probation

---

4   One officer who worked with homeless offenders illustrated the translation of questions about physical hygiene into non-judgemental language, for example, "How often do you like to have a bath?".

5   Two annotated comments on forms illustrate how difficult it can be to reach a sound judgement when one has little way of corroborating what offenders say: "Substance misuse hard to assess at present, i.e. I doubt [the offender's] account." and "Not sure about stability of relationships - she's very reticent."

officers, we would summarise their preferences for a needs assessment scale as follows:

● a comprehensive rather than selective list of needs

● a form which can be shown to clients without difficulty

● a system requiring officers to tick a yes box, or no box for each need

● a form with a box adjacent to each need tickbox, allowing officers to write extra details

● a space for recording agreed actions with review columns to monitor the client's progress.

Statistical analysis of the forms

Some 1,500 forms were completed on almost 700 offenders at different stages in their supervision. The Simple, Intermediate and Complex Versions of the scale were completed by two teams each in Nottinghamshire Probation Service. One team in Middlesex Probation Service and one in Inner London Probation Service completed the Intermediate Version. Forms were completed on the majority of offenders in Nottinghamshire three times, at three-monthly intervals. Forms were completed twice on a smaller proportion of offenders in Middlesex[6] and ILPS. Table 2.1 summarises the number of offenders in each area for whom forms were completed.

Table 2.1 Numbers of offenders and completed forms

		Sweep 1	Sweep 2	Sweep 3
Simple Version	Notts	233	181	155
Intermediate Version	Notts	136	102	92
	ILPS	83	43	–
	Middlesex	95	21	–
Complex Version	Notts	159	130	95
	TOTAL	706	477	342

---

6   Excluding the pre-pilot carried out in Middlesex.

Figure 2.1

Profile of offender needs. Percentages of offenders with problems

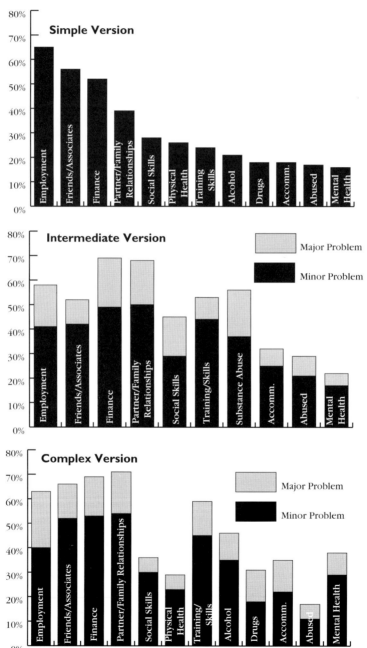

Profiles of need

Figure 2.1 summarises the profile of offender needs for each version of the form. The Figure shows levels of need as assessed when the first set of forms were completed. Full details are provided in Appendix Tables B1 to B3. Several points emerge from the Figure:

- problems with employment or finance were amongst the most commonly identified problem in all three versions of the form

- problems associated with criminal friends and with intimate family relationships were also commonly identified in all three versions

- problems with mental health, and with sexual, physical or racial abuse, were least often identified

- the prevalence of other needs varied across versions

- the 0/1 scoring in Version 1 resulted in less frequent identification of problems than the three-point scales in Versions 2 and 3.[7]

This profile of need is consistent with that emerging from the Home Office survey of offenders on probation (Mair and May, forthcoming). The survey found that 59% of males on probation were signed on as unemployed; 41 per cent had trouble paying essential bills; and 35 per cent had current debt problems. Two-fifths had a family member who had been convicted; three-quarters had friends in trouble with the law.

Changes over time

Three sets of forms were completed on 319 offenders, and two sets on 169. The time elapsing between completion of the first and the final form varied, but in most cases it was between four and six months. This is considerably shorter than the length of the average probation order, of course, and results cannot be used to indicate the extent to which needs were addressed over the entire period of supervision. However, the findings point to the order of magnitude, at least, of the level of change which can be expected, and also highlight problems in interpreting these changes.

The simplest way of presenting information on changes is to calculate an overall score for each offender, by summing scores on individual needs items. One can then examine differences over time in overall scores. Table 2.2 gives a breakdown by version, for the 488 offenders with at least two assessments, of proportions whose score improved, worsened or stayed the

---

7   One possible explanation for this is that the binary scoring system winnowed minor problems which were insufficiently serious to demand attention.

same between their first and final assessment. It is also possible to present average needs scores for different groups, allowing changes in the average to be highlighted. Table 2.3 does this, showing average scores for the three versions of the scale, on the first and final assessment. It also shows the percentage change over this period in average scores. Changes in scores for specific items are presented in Appendix B, Tables B4 to B6.

Table 2.2 Changes in needs scores: differences between first and final assessments

	version		
	Simple	Intermediate	Complex
Changes in Score	%	%	%
Improved	36	36	51
Stayed the same	44	33	22
Got worse	20	31	27
	100	100	100
Number of Offenders	189	153	132

Table 2.3 Average needs scores: first and final assessments

	version		
	Simple	Intermediate	Complex
First assessment	3.83	5.49	17.62
Final assessment	3.53	5.57	15.26
Percentage improvement	8%	–1%	13%
Number of Offenders	189	153	132

Table 2.2 shows that problems lessened, grew and remained unchanged in roughly equal proportions. Offenders for whom the complex scale was completed most often showed improvements (51%). Least change was shown in the simple version. Table 2.3 shows that overall scores improved for both the simple and complex versions, but deteriorated slightly for the intermediate version.[8] There is an apparent inconsistency for the intermediate version between Tables 2.2 and 2.3, in that more offenders improved than worsened, yet the average needs score deteriorated. The explanation is that the average size of deterioration was larger than the average size of improvement for the two groups.

Real deterioration?

The fact that problems were apparently exacerbated in around a quarter of offenders requires some explanation. Three things may have happened. First, the circumstances of some offenders certainly do worsen whilst under probation supervision. A conviction in court may trigger job-loss, for example, or separation from one's partner or homelessness – singly or in combination. Sometimes, the conviction may be a symptom of an increasingly chaotic lifestyle. One can safely assume that the proportion of cases where the deterioration is in any way linked to probation supervision is minimal.

Secondly, the scales will certainly be unreliable to some extent. That is, different probation officers will score the same level of need differently, and the same probation officer may give different scores at different times to the same level of need. Again, this is undoubtedly part of the explanation. It is noteworthy that the Simple Version, whose 0/1 scoring system allowed least scope for different scores, showed the smallest proportion of 'deteriorating' offenders.

Finally, as discussed earlier, disclosure of problems must, at least in a proportion of cases, increase over time. As probation officers get to know the offenders they supervise, they will be able to make a more accurate assessment of their problems.

Without a great deal of further research, it is impossible to disentangle fully the contribution made by each of these explanations to the phenomenon. However, some progress can be made by looking at those dimensions of need where improvement is possible, but not deterioration. Broadly speaking, people's levels of social skills, their employability, their academic and technical skills and problems arising from exposure to racial, sexual or physical abuse can improve but do not deteriorate over the life of a probation order. Table 2.4 shows that broadly similar proportions show worsening and improving need on these dimensions over the period of the research. In other words, the Table provides convincing evidence that the

---

8   Averages scores vary substantially between versions because of the different scoring systems.

apparent worsening of needs is an artefact of either score unreliability or fuller disclosure.

Furthermore, if one accepts that in general there is scope *only for improvement* on these dimensions of need, Table 2.4 provides circumstantial evidence that fuller disclosure is an important factor in explaining the apparent worsening of offenders' problems over time. The Table could be taken as showing that some net improvements occurred but these were counterbalanced by increased disclosure. We find this interpretation more plausible than the alternative, that there were neither improvements nor fuller disclosure, and that changes in both directions simply indicate the underliability of scales of this sort.

Table 2.4 Changes in selected dimensions of need

	Worsening	Improving	Number of Assessments
Need			
Social skills	8%	7%	488
Employability	8%	9%	483
Qualifications and skills	6%	3%	487
Racial/Sexual/ Physical abuse	3%	5%	482

3 Conclusions

Summary of key findings

This study has piloted three versions of a needs assessment scale for use by probation officers. The exercise has yielded findings both about the reception which such scales might receive amongst staff, and about the value of substantive results. The key points to emerge from the process of piloting the scales, and from feedback from probation officers about the scales, are:

- probation officers find no overwhelming difficulty in using needs assessment scales

- some find them useful as ways of structuring assessment

- many are less convinced about their potential for improving practice

- some found the classifications over-simplified

- there were some anxieties that scales might de-skill probation staff and erode their autonomy.

Some 1,500 forms were completed on almost 700 offenders at different stages in their supervision. Forms were completed more than once for almost 500 of the 700 offenders. Substantive findings about levels of need amongst this groups include:

- Problems with employment or finance were the most commonly identified problem in all three versions of the form.

- Problems associated with criminal friends and with intimate family relationships were commonly identified in all three versions.

- Problems with mental health, and with sexual, physical or racial abuse, were less often identified.

- Large minorities, or in one version, just over half, of offenders showed improvements in problems over time.

- Large minorities of offenders also showed no change.

- Large minorities of offenders showed apparent worsening of problems over time.

- This deterioration is best explained as an artefact of fuller disclosure over time, or as a product of variations in the definition of problems.

Policy implications

These findings have various implications for the development of needs assessment scales. They raise general issues about reconciling the demands for good-quality management information with the realities of professional practice, and more specific issues about the design of scales.

Reconciling the need for management information with professional practice

A central finding of this study is that successful implementation of a national needs assessment scale will need carefully planned implementation. Service managers face a choice between imposing a data collection system, and designing one which generates management information in the process of use as a practice tool. The more that management information is produced as a by-product of everyday work processes, the more accurate and reliable it will be. If data collection systems are 'bolted on' to probation work processes rather than integrated into them, the quality of the resultant data will be patchy without constant management intervention. In the language of quality management, therefore, one needs to achieve quality assurance by getting the processes right, rather than impose quality controls on processes which are poorly suited to generate management information.

Given the concerns of probation officers, careful planning is needed for the introduction of any needs assessment scale. The various rationales for the scale need to be explained, and evidence of its value presented. Staff will need persuading that scales can:

- support rather than erode professionalism

- improve consistency of assessment

- produce a more equitable service

- helping to chart the work of the service

- demonstrate probation effectiveness.

Checklist or validated diagnostic scale?

Throughout the research main-grade and senior officers emphasised the complexity of assessing offenders' needs. We agree, and think that it is more realistic to conceptualise needs assessment scales in the probation setting as devices to structure assessment, rather than as diagnostic tools. We think that if a scale were complex enough to capture the full complexity of offenders' needs it would be too time-consuming to complete.

Certainly there are occasions where properly validated specialist assessment tests would be useful for assessing specific problems, such as illiteracy or drug or alcohol dependence (cf Roberts, 1995). However, we are sceptical of the value (or even practicability) of developing a comprehensive diagnostic scale covering the full range of problems which offenders present. It is also worth recognising that the checklist approach poses less of an obvious threat to professional autonomy. Given the growing popularity of the LSI-R scale, it is worth pointing out that it is no more a tool for diagnosing *need* than the scales which we piloted; what it does do, however – and apparently very well (see Gendreau et al., 1995) - is to combine judgements about need in a way which yields an assessment of the risk of reconviction. We shall return to this below.

Measuring needs

A related issue is the extent to which needs assessment scales should try to chart the intensity of need. The difficulty of finding any objective way of differentiating between levels of high, medium and low need convinces us that the attempt should not even be made. This research indicates that the best option would be to use a simple binary classification system, in which officers have to decide whether or not a need should be addressed in the course of supervision. This ties the scoring system to decisions which actually have to be made, instead of imposing a veneer of objectivity on a judgement which is inevitably subjective. We think that this approach would actually give more meaning to management information about needs than a more elaborate scoring system. However, if priority is attached to the objective measurement on need, there is no alternative except to develop fully validated tests for each dimension of need which is to be measured.

A particular advantage of using a binary scoring system of this sort is that it should dovetail easily with the work of probation officers in preparing PSRs and in drawing up supervision plans. For the judgements which officers have to make at these stages are less about the intensity of need, and more about whether action is required to address the need. Many probation areas use checklists in preparing PSRs; some are now using forms to record supervision plans which include lists of needs to be addressed in the course of supervision; these lists differ little from those on our piloted forms.

A final consideration is that any system for collecting information on offender needs on a national basis should be compatible with local systems. Those probation areas which have opted for more elaborate classification systems would be readily able to convert their scores into the national binary 'currency'. If however the national system involved scoring needs on three- or five-point scales, it would be incompatible with simpler systems. The introduction of a national computerised case-management system will, of course, put a premium on such compatibility.

Dimensions of need

The original specification for the pilot included testing out a very simple scale, with three key dimensions of need. In the event, the pre-pilot design phase suggested that this would not be a realistic proposition, and this was confirmed when it proved impossible to 'market' this scale to any of the teams which were taking part. A scale limited to three dimensions would have no credibility with users whatsoever.

Leaving aside problems of implementation, we agree with the adage that 'what gets measured gets done'. Including a sub-set of needs in a scale would undoubtedly skew practice towards addressing these needs and ignoring others. At present, there is an insufficiently sound knowledge base for advocating heavy selectivity in the items to be covered by a scale.

What needs should be included in a scale is partly an empirical issue (see Mair and May, forthcoming) and partly a matter for professional judgement. As researchers we are hesitant to offer a definitive list of needs to be included in a scale, though we think the following should be included:

- the adequacy of training/academic qualifications

- employability and employment issues

- accommodation

- financial management

- life Skills

- mental disturbance

- physical health

- the influence of criminally-involved friends and associates

- family/partner relationships

- drug misuse

- alcohol misuse

- racial abuse

- sexual or physical abuse

- offence-specific problems not already covered

- other needs.

Needs and risk of reconviction

At the time that this research was being completed, the Home Office's Offender Group Reconviction Score (OGRS) was being finalised. At the same time several probation areas were beginning to experiment with the Canadian LSI-R scale, which combines assessment of risk and need. Whatever precise approach is taken to the assessment of need, it obviously makes sense to ensure that this is properly integrated with assessing risk of reconviction.

There are two broad approaches. The first is to combine the sort of scale which we have piloted with OGRS. If this were done, the score for risk of reconviction would be calculated independently of needs, as OGRS relies only on demographic and criminal history variables in calculating its score. Probation officers would thus make their professional judgement about risk in the light of the OGRS score on the one hand, and their assessment of need on the other. The alternative is to use a system such as LSI-R. In this, assessment of needs and risk is interwoven, as the risk score is derived in part from needs variables. LSI-R is one such option. Alternatively, an actuarial scale could be constructed much as OGRS but including variables measuring needs.

Whether OGRS is a better predictor of risk than scales which incorporate needs variables is an empirical issue. Sutton and Davies (1996) argue that OGRS' reliance on 'static' risk factors (which are not subject to change) makes it reasonably accurate in predicting risks for groups as small as 50 offenders, but inaccurate in assessing risk in individual case situations. We think that scales which include needs variables (or 'dynamic' variables) may turn out to be equally imprecise. Whatever the basis of the reconviction score, probation officers will be required to exercise their judgement in assessing whether the offender in question belongs to the x per cent which will get reconvicted or the 100 - x per cent who will not. What is needed is an empirical test of the proposition that scales including needs variables are more precise than those which do not.

Whatever the outcome, we think that risks/needs scales such as LSI-R have a lot to recommend them; it is also clear that this particular scale is compatible with simpler binary scales of the sort which we have piloted.

A 'value-added' measure - assessing improvement

When the research was commissioned, it was envisaged that comparing scores on a needs assessment scale at the start and end of supervision would enable the construction of a performance indicator reflecting the 'value added' by probation supervision. Such a performance indicator might be of use both for front-line supervisors reviewing the performance of their staff, and for more senior managers and the Home Office. In principle, for example, it would be possible to compare different teams' or probation areas' aggregate improvement in scores.

The findings of this study do not rule out such a performance indicator, but they do point to some limitations. Certainly, the scale scores cannot be taken at face value. In some cases, fuller disclosure over time will mean that some offenders' problems are apparently exacerbated over time. Scale unreliability will also mean that the apparent development – or solution – of problems is in some cases illusory. In some cases, too, offenders' problems will genuinely get worse – or better – for reasons which may be unrelated to probation supervision. All these factors will combine to ensure the impossibility of knowing whether lack of change over time in average needs scores actually masks an improvement, or whether a five per cent gain is actually a substantial improvement.

These obstacles should not be overstated. Plenty of other public sector performance indicators have similar limitations, without being thereby rendered useless. Most public sector performance indicators by their nature cannot measure performance definitively, but simply raise questions for further examination. It would be possible to construct a value-added measure. It might well point to differences in performance which would repay closer examination, but there would be considerable difficulties in interpreting such differences – as well as presentational ones in explaining that small improvements were actually large ones.

One final problem deserves careful consideration. If probation areas' performance was being judged even indirectly by HM Inspectorate of Probation by reference to changes in average scores on a needs scale, probation officers would find themselves under pressure to cheat by massaging their performance. This would almost certainly happen if officers benefited personally – for example through performance-related pay. But even if the benefits were only indirect – where for example high-performing areas gained in terms of specific grant allocation – manipulation of the scores would rapidly become institutionalised amongst the entire workforce.

We think that there may be some mileage in exploring another approach to assessing the gains achieved through probation supervision. This would involve getting officers to assess what improvements had been achieved by the end of supervision. At PSR stage and when drawing up a supervision plan, officers need to score offenders on whether a need requires addressing or not. At the conclusion of the order – or during quarterly reviews - a similar form should be used to assess whether the offender's various needs have been reduced as a result of probation effort. SPOs would have an important part to play in validating these assessments. The approach has two advantages over a 'before-and-after' score comparison:

- it would provide a mechanism for disregarding changes which are unrelated to supervision

- manipulation of scores would be much more transparent.

As with 'before-and-after' comparisons of needs scores, such a system would be highly subject to manipulation if it were used to distribute organisational rewards or resources. Using any 'value added' measure to link performance to resources would have highly perverse effects in the probation context.

For all the problems involved, we think that there is an overwhelming case for collecting information in a structured and consistent manner on the extent to which offenders needs have been addressed. By assessing offenders' needs consistently and by measuring success in addressing these needs, the service will be making a powerful statement to all probation stakeholders about its central purpose.

Annex A: The three versions of the needs assessment scale

Notes to Probation Officers – how to use the Needs Assessment Scales.

When to complete the Needs Assessment Scale: the Needs Assessment Scales should be completed at the start of a probation order, at 3 months and again at 6 months for new clients. Needs Assessment Scales for existing clients should be completed in the first week of January, in the first week of April and finally in the first week of July.

Scoring: the most appropriate score should be entered in the right hand column; please choose the description which best describes yout client even if it is not an exact description. Please do not leave the category blank.

Categorising the information – please use your professional judgement: the information given by the offender should form the basis of the Needs Assessment. It is your interpretation of the information and your opinion which should be recorded; with the exception to this is *Accommodation* where the offender's opinion of the suitability of accommodation should determine the score.

Verifying the information: where relevant please try to check the information given by or about the offender against details in her/his file e.g. past or third party information on mental health and abuse.

Please refer to the full explanations of the categories before using the Needs Assessment Scale.

Needs Assessment Scale - **Simple Version**   **1**

CRN		Client's initials	First name	
DOB	Male/female	EMO1code	Team	
PO's name		Date of order		Termination date

Score

Academic/ vocational skills	No problems with literacy/ numeracy or has qualifications	0	Problems with literacy/ numeracy; no qualifications	1	
Employment	Employed or no problems finding work	0	Unemployed/cannot find work/needs training	1	

Accommodation	Satisfactory permanent or temporary accommodation	0	Unsatisfactory or homeless	1	

Financial management	Can manage finances	0	Has financial problems	1	

Social skills	Good social skills	0	Would benefit from social skills training	1	

Mental health	No problems or none disclosed	0	Mental health problems which affect functioning	1	
Physical health	No problems/rarely ill	0	Sporadic or chronic ill health	1	

Friends/ associates	Friends/associates not involved in crime	0	Some/all friends or associates are involved in crime	1	
Partner/family relationships	Satisfactory and stable	0	Unstable and/or partner/family member has substance abuse or mental health problems	1	

Racial, sexual or physical abuse	No evidence of abuse	0	Present or past abuse causing problems	1	

Alcohol misuse	Controlled use; does not affect functioning	0	Misuse/dependency causing legal, social or financial problems	1	
Drug misuse	Controlled use(or none), does not affect functioning	0	Misuse/dependency causing legal, social or financial problems	1	

Date completed						PO's comments

In addition please tick appropriate column

Motivation to stop offending	Wants to take action to stop offending	Ambivalent about the need to stop offending; lacks motivation	Does not want to stop offending. Unco-operative

Needs Assessment Scale - **Intermediate Version** 2

CRN	Client's initials	First name
Male/Female	**DOB**	**EMO1 code**	**Team**
PO's name		**Date of order**	**Termination date**

Academic/ vocational skills	Completed 5th year with CSE/ O level/GCSE/NVQs **0**	No qualifications/ low skills - causing **1** minor problems	Severe problems with literacy /numeracy. **2** Lacks basic life skills	
Employment	Employed or no problems finding work **0**	Poor job history, may lack skills or need training **1**	Job prospects minimal, lacks skills or **2** motivation	
Accommodation	Satisfactory permanent or temporary **0** accommodation	Not satisfactory, but acceptable until **1** something better is found	Homeless or unsatisfactory **2** accommodation	
Financial management	No problems/ financially **0** competent	Temporary or minor difficulties **1**	Severe difficulties: debt, county court **2** judgements etc	
Social skills	Good social skills **0**	Would benefit from social skills training **1**	Serious social skills deficits. Needs **2** social skills training.	
Mental health	No problems **0**	Minor problems or more serious ones **1** controlled by treatment	Serious problems- needs treatment **2**	
Friends/ associates	Friends/associates are not involved **0** in crime	Some friends/associates are involved in crime **1**	Most friends/ associates are involved in crime **2**	
Partner/ family relationships	Satisfactory and stable **0**	Some problems with relationships **1**	Is in unstable or can't form stable **2** relationships	
Substance misuse	No use/controlled use of substances does **0** not impair functioning	Occasional misuse, some functional impairment/ **1** receiving treatment	Uncontrolled misuse of substances/ **2** dependency; needs treatment	
Racial, sexual or physical abuse	No evidence of abuse **0**	Present or past abuse causing some **1** problems	Serious problems which need addressing **2**	

Date completed						**PO's comments**

In addition please tick appropriate column

Motivation to stop offending	Wants to take action to stop offending	Ambivalent about the need to stop offending, lacks motivation	Does not want to stop offending. Unco-operative

35

Needs Assessment Scale - **Complex Version**   **3**

CRN		Client's initials		First name	
Male/Female	DOB		EMO1 code	Team	
PO's name		Date of order		Termination date	

Score

Academic/ vocational skills	Completed 5th year with CSE/ O level/GCSE/NVQs **0**	No qualifications/ low skills - causing **1** minor problems	Severe problems with literacy /numeracy. **3** Lacks basic life skills	
Employment	Employed or no problems finding work **0**	Poor job history, may lack skills or need training **3**	Job prospects minimal, lacks skills or **6** motivation	

Accommodation	Satisfactory permanent or temporary **0** accommodation	Not satisfactory, but acceptable until **3** something better is found	Homeless or unsatisfactory **6** accommodation	

Financial management	No problems/ financially **0** competent	Temporary or minor difficulties **3**	Severe difficulties: debt, county court **5** judgements etc	

Social skills	Good social skills **0**	Would benefit from social skills training **3**	Serious social skills deficits. Needs social **5** skills training.	

Mental health	No problems **0**	Minor problems or more serious ones **3** controlled by treatment	Serious problems- needs treatment **6**	
Physical health	No problems/ rarely ill **0**	Disability/ illness regularly limits functioning **1**	Serious disability/ chronic illness- needs **2** frequent medical care	

Friends/ associates	Friends/associates are not involved incrime **0**	Some friends/associates are involved in crime **2**	Most friends/ associates are involved in crime **4**	
Partner/family relationships	Satisfactory and stable **0**	Some problems with relationships **3**	Is in unstable or can't form stable **5** relationships	

Alcohol misuse	Controlled use of alcohol does **0** not impair functioning	Occasional misuse, some functional impairment/ **3** receiving treatment	Uncontrolled misuse/ dependency; needs **6** treatment	
Drug misuse	No use/controlled use of substances; **0**	Occasional misuse, some functional impairment/ **3** receiving treatment	Uncontrolled misuse/ dependency; needs **6** treatment	

Racial, sexual or physical abuse	No evidence of abuse **0**	Present or past abuse causing some **2** problems	Serious problems which need addressing **4**	

Date completed					PO's comments	

In addition please tick appropriate column

Motivation to stop offending	*Wants to take action to stop offending*	*Ambivalent about the need to stop offending; lacks motivation*	*Does not want to stop offending. Unco-operative*

Annex B: Supplementary tables

Table B1

Percentage of offenders with needs: simple version

	No Problem	Problem	Total
	%	%	%
Academic and vocational skills	76	24	100
Employability	35	65	100
Accommodation	82	18	100
Finance	48	52	100
Social skills	72	28	100
Mental health	84	16	100
Physical health	74	26	100
Associates	44	56	100
Relationships	61	39	100
Race/Sex abuse	83	17	100
Alcohol misuse	79	21	100
Drug misuse	82	18	100

Total in sample: 233 offenders, all from Nottinghamshire

Table B2

Percentage of offenders with needs: intermediate version

	No problem %	Bit of problem %	Serious problem %	Total %
Academic & vocational skills	46	44	9	100
Employabilty	42	41	17	100
Accommodation	69	25	7	100
Finance	31	49	20	100
Social Skills	65	29	6	100
Mental Health	79	17	5	100
Associates	47	42	10	100
Relaltionships	33	50	18	100
Substance Misuse	45	37	19	100
Race/Sex abuse	72	21	8	100

Total in Sample: 136 offenders (Nottinghamshire)
83 offenders (ILPS)
95 offenders (Middlesex)

Table B3

Percentage of offenders with need: complex version

	No problem %	Bit of problem %	Serious problem %	Total %
Academic & Vocational skills	41	45	14	100
Employability	37	40	23	100
Accommodation	65	22	13	100
Finance	31	53	16	100
Social Skills	64	30	6	100
Mental Health	62	29	9	100
Physical Health	71	23	6	100
Associates	33	52	14	100
Relationships	29	54	17	100
Alcohol Misuse	53	35	11	100
Drug Misuse	69	18	13	100
Race/Sex abuse	82	11	6	100

Total in sample: 159 offenders (all Nottinghamshire)

Table B4

Score difference between first and last assessment: simple version

	Number	%
Academic & Vocational Skills		
New problem	6	3
No problem	137	72
Problem the same	43	23
Problem gone	3	2
Employability		
New problem	6	3
No problem	59	31
Problem the same	113	60
Problem gone	11	6
Accommodation		
New problem	13	7
No problem	142	75
Problem the same	16	8
Problem gone	18	10
Finance		
New problem	9	5
No problem	81	43
Problem the same	74	39
Problem gone	25	13
Social Skills		
New problem	9	5
No problem	131	69
Problem the same	39	21
Problem gone	10	5
Mental Health		
New problem	5	3
No problem	152	80
Problem the same	25	13
Problem gone	7	4

Continued

Physical Health

New problem	6	3
No problem	128	68
Problem the same	47	25
Problem gone	7	4

Associates

New problem	5	3
No problem	76	40
Problem the same	93	49
Problem gone	15	8

Relationships

New problem	6	3
No problem	108	58
Problem the same	57	30
Problem gone	16	9

Race/Sex Abuse

New problem	4	2
No problem	154	82
Problem the same	24	13
Problem gone	6	3

Alcohol Misuse

New problem	6	3
No problem	140	74
Problem the same	33	17
Problem gone	10	5

Drug Misuse

New problem	4	2
No problem	153	81
Problem the same	23	12
Problem gone	9	5

Notes:
1. Number of offenders: 189
2. Where a third form was completed, this is compared to the first. Otherwise, the second is compared to the first.

Table B5

Score difference between first and last assessment: Intermediate version

	Number	%
Training/Skills		
No problem	71	43
Problem better	6	4
Problem worse	1	1
New problem	13	8
Problem the same	74	45
Employability		
No problem	51	32
Problem better	20	13
Problem worse	8	5
New problem	17	11
Problem the same	64	40
Accommodation		
No problem	86	52
Problem better	21	13
Problem worse	1	1
New problem	21	13
Problem the same	36	22
Finance		
No problem	43	26
Problem better	28	17
Problem worse	6	4
New problem	13	18
Problem the same	76	46
Social Skills		
No problem	100	61
Problem better	15	9
Problem worse	2	1
New problem	19	12
Problem the same	29	18

Continued

Mental Health

No problem	121	73
Problem better	15	9
Problem worse	2	1
New problem	6	4
Problem the same	21	13

Associates

No problem	72	44
Problem better	16	10
Problem worse	9	5
New problem	15	9
Problem the same	53	32

Relationships

No problem	47	29
Problem better	26	16
Problem worse	5	3
New problem	10	6
Problem the same	76	46

Substance Abuse

No problem	70	43
Problem better	25	15
Problem worse	6	4
New problem	8	5
Problem the same	55	34

Race/Sex Abuse

No problem	110	68
Problem better	9	6
Problem worse	3	2
New problem	4	2
Problem the same	35	22

Notes:

1. Number of offenders: 165
2. Where a third form was completed, this is compared to the first. Otherwise, the second is compared to the first.

Table B6
Score difference between first and last assessment: Complex Version

	Number	%
Training/Skills		
No problem	55	41
Problem better	4	3
Problem worse	3	2
New problem	2	2
Problem the same	69	52
Employability		
No problem	44	33
Problem better	14	10
Problem worse	3	2
New problem	4	3
Problem the same	69	51
Accommodation		
No problem	79	59
Problem better	23	17
Problem worse	4	3
New problem	12	9
Problem the same	16	12
Finance		
No problem	36	27
Problem better	24	18
Problem worse	4	3
New problem	7	5
Problem the same	63	47
Social Skills		
No problem	83	62
Problem better	10	7
Problem worse	6	4
New problem	2	1
Problem the same	33	25
Mental Health		
No problem	83	62
Problem better	11	8
Problem worse	4	3
New problem	2	1
Problem the same	34	25

Continued

Physical Health

No problem	91	68
Problem better	6	4
Problem worse	3	2
New problem	6	4
Problem the same	28	21

Associates

No problem	37	28
Problem better	21	16
Problem worse	3	2
New problem	4	3
Problem the same	69	51

Relationships

No problem	34	25
Problem better	28	21
Problem worse	4	3
New problem	6	4
Problem the same	62	46

Alcohol Misuse

No problem	65	49
Problem better	23	17
Problem worse	1	1
New problem	7	5
Problem the same	38	28

Drug Misuse

No problem	84	63
Problem better	20	15
New problem	5	4
Problem the same	25	19

Race/Sex Abuse

No problem	109	82
Problem better	7	5
New problem	5	4
Problem the same	12	9

Notes:
1. Number of offenders: 134
2. Where a third form was completed, this is compared to the first.
   Otherwise, the second is compared to the first.

References

Andrews, D.A. Zinger, I., Hoge, R.D., Bonta, J., Gendreau, P. and Cullen, F.T. (1990). *'Does correctional treatment work? A criminologically relevant and psychologically informed meta-analysis'.* Criminology, 28, 3, 369 - 403.

Andrews, D. and Bonta, J. (1995). *LSI-R: The Level of Service Inventory - Revised.* Toronto: Multi-Health Systems Inc.

Bonta, J., Pang, B., Parkinson, P., Barkwell, L. and Wallace-Capretta, S. (1994). *The Revised Manitoba Classification System for Probationers.* Manitoba: Manitoba Justice Department.

Burnett, R., (1996). *Fitting supervision to offenders: assessment and allocation decisions in the Probation Service.* Home Office Research Study No 153. London: Home Office.

Copas, J. (1994). *'On using crime statistics for prediction'*, in Statistics of Crime, M Walker (ed.). Oxford: Oxford University Press.

Farrington, D. (1994). *'Human development and criminal careers'*, in Maguire, M., Morgan, R. and Reiner, R. The Oxford Handbook of Criminology. Oxford: Oxford University Press.

Gendreau, P., Little, T. and Coggin, C. (1992). *A Meta-analysis of the Predictors of Adult Offender Recidivism: assessment guidelines for classification and treatment.* Ottawa: Paper submitted to the Corrections Branch of the Office of the Solicitor General.

Home Office (1995). *National Standards for the Supervision of Offenders in the Community.* London: Home Office.

Humphrey, C., Carter, P. and Pease, K. (1992). *'A reconviction predictor for probationers'.* British Journal of Social Work 22, 33 - 46.

Kemshall, H. (1996). *Reviewing risk: a review of research on the assessment and management of risk and dangerousness - implications for policy and practice in the probation service.* A report for the Home Office Research and Statistics Directorate. London: Home Office.

Lipsey, M. (1991). *'Juvenile delinquency treatment: a meta-analytic inquiry into the variability of effects',* in T.D. Cook, H. Cooper, D.S. Cordray et al. (eds.). *Meta-analysis for Explanation: A Casebook.* New York, Russell Sage.

Losel, F. (1995). *'The efficacy of correctional treatment: a review and synthesis of meta-evaluations',* in McGuire, J. (ed.)*What works? Reducing reoffending.* Chichester: Wiley.

McGuire, J. (ed.)*What works? Reducing reoffending.* Chichester: Wiley.

Mair, G. and May, C. (forthcoming). *Offenders on Probation.* Home Office Research Study No 167. London: Home Office.

NACRO (1993). *Community Care and Mentally Disturbed Offenders.* NACRO Mental Health Advisory Committee Policy Paper No 1. London: NACRO.

Nottinghamshire Probation Service (1996). *Annual Report.* Nottingham: Nottinghamshire Probation Service.

Roberts, C. (1995). *'Effective practice and service delivery',* in McGuire, J. (ed.)*What works? Reducing reoffending.* Chichester: Wiley.

Sutton, D. and Davies, P. (1996). *An introduction to the "Level of Service Inventory - Revised"* (LSI-R). Cardiff: Cognitive Centre Foundation.

Wilkinson, C., Buckley, K. and Symes, C. (1995). *Dealing with Women: a needs analysis in relation to the probation service.* A report to the Home Office Research and Planning Unit.

Publications

List of research publications

A list of research reports for the last three years is provided below. A **full** list of publications is available on request from the Research and Statistics Directorate Information & Publications Group.

Home Office Research Studies (HORS)

133. **Intensive Probation in England and Wales: an evaluation.** George Mair, Charles Lloyd, Claire Nee and Rae Sibbett. 1994. xiv + 143pp. (0 11 341114 6).

134. **Contacts between Police and Public: findings from the 1992 British Crime Survey.** Wesley G Skogan. 1995. ix + 93pp. (0 11 341115 4).

135. **Policing low-level disorder: Police use of Section 5 of the Public Order Act 1986.** David Brown and Tom Ellis. 1994. ix + 69pp. (0 11 341116 2).

136. **Explaining reconviction rates: A critical analysis.** Charles Lloyd, George i and Mike Hough. 1995. xiv + 103pp. (0 11 341117 0).

137. **Case Screening by the Crown Prosecution Service: How and why cases are terminated.** Debbie Crisp and David Moxon. 1995. viii + 66pp. (0 11 341137 5).

138. **Public Interest Case Assessment Schemes.** Debbie Crisp, Claire Whittaker and Jessica Harris. 1995. x + 58pp. (0 11 341139 1).

139. **Policing domestic violence in the 1990s.** Sharon Grace. 1995. x + 74pp. (0 11 341140 5).140. **Young people, victimisation and the police: British Crime Survey findings on experiences and attitudes of 12 to 15 year olds.** Natalie Aye Maung. xii + 140pp.

141. **The Settlement of refugees in Britain.** Jenny Carey-Wood, Karen Duke, Valerie Karn and Tony Marshall. 1995. xii + 133pp. (0 11 341145 6).

142. **Vietnamese Refugees since 1982.** Karen Duke and Tony Marshall. 1995. x + 62pp. (0 11 341147 2).

143. **The Parish Special Constables Scheme.** Peter Southgate, Tom Bucke and Carole Byron. 1995. x + 59pp. (1 85893 458 3).

144. **Measuring the Satisfaction of the Courts with the Probation Service.** Chris May. 1995. x + 76pp. (1 85893 483 4).

145. **Young people and crime.** John Graham and Benjamin Bowling. 1995. 142pp. (1 85893 551 2).

146. **Crime against retail and manufacturing premises: findings from the 1994 Commercial Victimisation Survey.** Catriona Mirrlees-Black and Alec Ross. 1995. xi + 110pp. (1 85893 554 7).

147. **Anxiety about crime: findings from the 1994 British Crime Survey.** Michael Hough. 1995. viii + 92pp. (1 85893 553 9).

148. **The ILPS Methadone Prescribing Project.** Rae Sibbitt. 1996. viii + 69pp. (1 85893 485 0).

149. **To scare straight or educate? The British experience of day visits to prison for young people.** Charles Lloyd. 1996. xi + 60pp. (1 85893 643 5).

150. **Predicting reoffending for Discretionary Conditional Release.** John B Copas, Peter Marshall and Roger Tarling. 1996. vii + 49pp. (1 85893 576 8).

151. **Drug misuse declared: results of the 1994 British Crime Survey.** Malcolm Ramsay and Andrew Percy. 1996. xv + 131pp. (1 85893 628 4).

152. **An Evaluation of the Introduction and Operation of the Youth Court.** David O'Mahony and Kevin Haines. 1996. viii + 70pp. (1 85893 5792).

153. **Fitting supervision to offenders: assessment and allocation decisions in the Probation Service.** Ros Burnett. 1996. xi + 99pp. (1 85893 599 7).

Research and Planning Unit Papers (RPUP)

81. **The welfare needs of unconvicted prisoners.** Diane Caddle and Sheila White. 1994.

82. **Racially motivated crime: a British Crime Survey analysis.** Natalie Aye Maung and Catriona Mirrlees-Black. 1994.

83. **Mathematical models for forecasting Passport demand.** Andy Jones and John MacLeod. 1994.

84. **The theft of firearms.** John Corkery. 1994.

85. **Equal opportunities and the Fire Service.** Tom Bucke. 1994.

86. **Drug Education Amongst Teenagers: a 1992 British Crime Survey Analysis.** Lizanne Dowds and Judith Redfern. 1995.

87. **Group 4 Prisoner Escort Service: a survey of customer satisfaction.** Claire Nee. 1994.

88. **Special Considerations: Issues for the Management and Organisation of the Volunteer Police.** Catriona Mirrlees-Black and Carole Byron. 1995.

89. **Self-reported drug misuse in England and Wales: findings from the 1992 British Crime Survey.** Joy Mott and Catriona Mirrlees-Black. 1995.

90. **Improving bail decisions: the bail process project, phase 1.** John Burrows, Paul Henderson and Patricia Morgan. 1995.

91. **Practitioners' views of the Criminal Justice Act: a survey of criminal justice agencies.** George Mair and Chris May. 1995.

92. **Obscene, threatening and other troublesome telephone calls to women in England and Wales: 1982-1992.** Wendy Buck, Michael Chatterton and Ken Pease. 1995.

93. **A survey of the prisoner escort and custody service provided by Group 4 and by Securicor Custodial Services.** Diane Caddle. 1995.

Research Findings

8.   **Findings from the International Crime Survey.** Pat Mayhew. 1994.

9   **Fear of Crime: Findings from the 1992 British Crime Survey.** Catriona Mirrlees-Black and Natalie Aye Maung. 1994.

10.   **Does the Criminal Justice system treat men and women differently?** Carol Hedderman and Mike Hough. 1994.

11.   **Participation in Neighbourhood Watch: Findings from the 1992 British Crime Survey.** Lizanne Dowds and Pat Mayhew. 1994.

12.   **Explaining Reconviction Rates: A Critical Analysis.** Charles Lloyd, George Mair and Mike Hough. 1995.

13.   **Equal opportunities and the Fire Service.** Tom Bucke. 1994.

14.   **Trends in Crime: Findings from the 1994 British Crime Survey.** Pat Mayhew, Catriona Mirrlees-Black and Natalie Aye Maung. 1994.

15.   **Intensive Probation in England and Wales: an evaluation.** George Mair, Charles Lloyd, Claire Nee and Rae Sibbett. 1995.

16.   **The settlement of refugees in Britain.** Jenny Carey-Wood, Karen Duke, Valerie Karn and Tony Marshall. 1995.

17.   **Young people, victimisation and the police: British Crime Survey findings on experiences and attitudes of 12 to 15 year olds.** Natalie Aye Maung.

18.   **Vietnamese Refugees since 1982.** Karen Duke and Tony Marshall. 1995.

19.   **Supervision of Restricted Patients in the Community.** Suzanne Dell and Adrian Grounds. 1995.

20.   **Videotaping children's evidence: an evaluation.** Graham Davies, Clare Wilson, Rebecca Mitchell and John Milsom. 1995.

21.   **The mentally disordered and the police.** Graham Robertson, Richard Pearson and Robert Gibb. 1995.

22. **Preparing records of taped interviews.** Andrew Hooke and Jim Knox. 1995.

23. **Obscene, threating and other troublesome telephone calls to women: Findings from the British Crime Survey.** Wendy Buck, Michael Chatterton and Ken Pease. 1995.

24. **Young people and crime.** John Graham and Ben Bowling. 1995.

25. **Anxiety about crime: Findings from the 1994 British Crime Survey.** Michael Hough. 1995.

26. **Crime against retail premises in 1993.** Catriona Mirrlees-Black and Alec Ross. 1995.

27. **Crime against manufacturing premises in 1993.** Catriona Mirrlees-Black and Alec Ross. 1995.

28. **Policing and the public: findings from the 1994 British Crime Survey.** Tom Bucke. 1995.

29. **The Child Witness Pack – An Evaluation.** Joyce Plotnikoff and Richard Woolfson. 1995.

30. **To scare straight or educate? The British experience of day visits to prison for young people**. Charles Lloyd. 1996.

31. **The ADT drug treatment programme at HMP Downview - a preliminary evaluation.** Elaine Player and Carol Martin. 1996.

32. **Wolds remand prison - an evaluation.** Keith Bottomley, Adrian James, Emma Clare and Alison Liebling. 1996.

33. **Drugs misuse declared: results of the 1994 British Crime Survey.** Malcolm Ramsay and Andrew Percy. 1996.

34. **Crack cocaine and drugs-crime careers.** Howard Parker and Tim Bottomley. 1996.

Research Bulletin

The Research Bulletin is published periodically and contains short articles on recent research.

Occasional Papers

Measurement of caseload weightings associated with the Children Act. Richard J. Gadsden and Graham J. Worsdale. 1994. (Available from the RSD Information Section.)

Managing difficult prisoners: The Lincoln and Hull special units. Professor Keith Bottomley, Professor Norman Jepson, Mr Kenneth Elliott and Dr Jeremy Coid. 1994. (Available from RSD Information Section.)

The Nacro diversion initiative for mentally disturbed offenders: an account and an evaluation. Home Office, NACRO and Mental Health Foundation. 1994. (Available from RSD Information Section.)

Probation Motor Projects in England and Wales. J P Martin and Douglas Martin. 1994.

Community-based treatment of sex offenders: an evaluation of seven treatment programmes. R Beckett, A Beech, D Fisher and A S Fordham. 1994.

Videotaping children's evidence: an evaluation. Graham Davies, Clare Wilson, Rebecca Mitchell and John Milsom. 1995.

Managing the needs of female prisoners. Allison Morris, Chris Wilkinson, Andrea Tisi, Jane Woodrow and Ann Rockley. 1995.

Local information points for volunteers. Michael Locke, Nick Richards, Lorraine Down, Jon Griffish and Roger Worgan. 1995.

Requests for Publications

Home Office Research Studies from 143 onwards, *Research and Planning Unit Papers, Research Findings and Research Bulletins* are available on request from:

Research and Statistics Directorate
Information and Publications Group
Room 1308, Apollo House
36 Wellesley Road
Croydon
CR9 3RR
Telephone: 0181-760 8340 (answerphone)

Internet: http//www.open.gov.uk/home_off/rsd/rsdhome.htp
E-mail: rsd.ha apollo @ gtne.gov.uk.

Occasional Papers can be purchased from:
Home Office
Publications Unit
50 Queen Anne's Gate
London SW1H 9AT
Telephone: 0171 273 2302

Home Office Research Studies prior to 143 can be purchased from:

HMSO Publications Centre

(Mail, fax and telephone orders only)
PO Box 276, London SW8 5DT
Telephone orders: 0171-873 9090
General enquiries: 0171-873 0011
(queuing system in operation for both numbers)
Fax orders: 0171-873 8200

*And also from **HMSO Bookshops***